Historic Oxford

Written by
Richard Frost, M.A., D.Phil.

'What makes Oxford so beautiful', it has been said, 'is that it has retained so many buildings of an age of architectural perfection *in so small a space*.' Most of those buildings belong to the University or the colleges. Geographical considerations and earlier history made Oxford and not some other town the home of England's first university. In the early Middle Ages rivers provided the easiest means of transport and the Thames, rising in the western Cotswolds and flowing south-east to the sea beyond London, was a main artery of trade in southern England. Bridge building was in its infancy in England, but at Oxford a spit of gravel and shallow water made it possible for men and oxen to ford the river to Hinksey. This ford was at the south-western corner of a rectangle of land formed by the Thames, which made a turn to the south two miles upstream and then resumed its easterly course, and its tributary the Cherwell coming down from the north. This rectangle is protected on three sides by water, and from the rivers the land rises gently and provided a site easy to defend, yet safe from flooding. King Alfred, who was born at Wantage fifteen miles from Oxford in 849, fortified it in his struggle against the Danish invaders of Anglo-Saxon England and the Anglo-Saxon Chronicle relates that King Edward took possession of it for defensive purposes in the year 912. It was possible to build a simple bridge across the Cherwell where Magdalen Bridge now stands and the road crossing it from the east met the road coming from Northampton and the north, crossing the Oxenford on its way to Abingdon and the south, at the point of the Quatre Voies, the four ways. This pattern still remains a thousand years later: the early tracks have become urban thoroughfares and the name Quatre Voies has slipped into Carfax.

Its geographical position in the centre of southern England gave Oxford a special importance among the small Anglo-Saxon trading centres. It was a natural site for a castle from which the Norman conquerors could keep the Saxon population in subjection. In 1071, only five years after the Conquest, Robert D'Oili built the tower and fortified the mound of Oxford Castle overlooking the Hinksey Ford. Of pre-Conquest building all that remains to be seen is the tower of St Michael-at-the-Northgate, but, in addition to Robert D'Oili's tower, scattered around the city are various pieces of Norman building, such as the south door of the later Gothic church of St Peter-in-the-East, now converted into a library for one of the colleges, St Edmund Hall, and Christ Church Cathedral, built as a monastery church in the twelfth century.

AMERICANS IN OXFORD.

1st American – 'Do you reckon this car will put us down at the famous Oxford University?'

2nd American – 'Hustle round Ma, our train leaves for Stratford in 30 minutes.'

Shortage of time is still a problem for many visitors (by courtesy of Oxfordshire County Libraries).

Le manque de temps est toujours un problème pour le touriste.

Zeitmangel ist das Problem vieler Besucher

From the early days, when King Alfred made it a fortress against the Danish invaders, the history of Oxford has been woven into the history of Britain. Soon after the Conquest a close association grew up between Oxford and the English kings. A few miles north of Oxford was the Forest of Wychwood, which became the favourite hunting forest of the Norman and Angevin kings, and Henry I built a hunting lodge at Woodstock. The road from London to Wychwood passed, and still passes, through Oxford. It crossed the Cherwell by the bridge built by D'Oili to supersede the earlier Saxon bridge and went down what is the present High Street to Carfax and then north up the present Cornmarket and St Giles, following two of the 'four ways'. Henry I built Beaumont Palace, near the present Worcester College, and there his great-grandson Richard I, Cœur de Lion, was born. It was at Oxford that, in 1141, King Stephen besieged the Empress Matilda in the castle from which she escaped, dressed all in white, over the snow-covered land and the frozen Thames to reach the castle at Wallingford. It was at Oxford that Simon de Montfort's 'Mad Parliament' met, and here the first Royal proclamation ever to be written in English was issued. It was at Oxford that Cranmer, the principal author of the Book of Common Prayer, which has enshrined the beliefs and liturgy of the Anglican communion throughout the world, was martyred during the reign of Mary Tudor and that Bishops Latimer and Ridley were burned at the stake for their steadfastness to the same faith. During the Civil War in the seventeenth century King Charles I made Oxford his headquarters for a time. He himself lived at Christ Church and his queen had her Court at Merton. In the garden of New College is a high mound which was constructed as an emplacement for a cannon to fire cannon balls over the city wall if the Parliamentary forces came right up to the city itself; but the king and his young son with a great cavalcade of horsemen and foot soldiers escaped early one morning from the beleaguered city across Port Meadow.

🇫🇷 C'est en partie à sa situation géographique qu'Oxford doit son titre de première université d'Angleterre. Son site légèrement surélevé et entouré d'eau de trois côtés – la Tamise et son affluent la Cherwell – était facile à défendre et à l'abri des inondations. Par ailleurs, à une époque où les ponts étaient rares, son gué sur la Tamise s'avéra d'une importance primordiale. Alfred le Grand (règne : 871–99) y édifia des fortifications et en l'an 912 Edouard l'Ancien occupa les lieux. La construction du premier pont sur la Cherwell permit le développement de grandes routes dont les deux principales formaient et forment encore le lieu dit des « Quatre Voies » (devenu en anglais moderne Carfax) situé en plein centre ville.

Overleaf: Oxford seen from Headington Hill at dusk, by Frederick Mackenzie (c. 1787–1854) ▶
(by courtesy of the Ashmolean Museum, Oxford).
Au verso: Oxford au crépuscule, vue de Headington Hill, par F. Mackenzie.
Umseitig: Oxford bei Dämmerung vom Headington Hügel gesehen.

Map of Oxford, 1578, by Ralph Agas (Bodl. Gough Maps Oxon. 1).

Carte d'Oxford établie par Ralph Agas en 1578.

Karte von Oxford von 1578 von Ralph Agas.

La position centrale d'Oxford au Sud de l'Angleterre lui fit également jouer, dès l'ère anglo-saxonne, un grand rôle commercial. Le seul vestige de cette époque est la tour de l'église St-Michael-at-the-Northgate. Peu après la conquête normande (1066), les fortifications et le donjon d'un château (œuvre de Robert d'Oili) furent édifiés. Ce donjon a survécu ainsi que, de la même époque, le portail Sud de l'église St-Peter-in-the-East (fin du gothique) et la cathédrale Christ Church (XIIe siècle).

Depuis l'époque d'Alfred le Grand, l'histoire d'Oxford a été intimement liée à celle des souverains anglais. A quelques kilomètres au Nord de la ville, la forêt de Wychwood devint le terrain de chasse favori des rois Normands puis des Plantagenêt après qu'Henri Ier (règne: 1100–35) y eut fait construire un pavillon de chasse. Henri Ier fit également édifier Beaumont Palace, lieu de naissance de son arrière-petit-fils Richard Ier, Cœur de Lion. C'est à Oxford aussi que le roi Etienne de Blois (règne : 1135–54) assiégea en 1141 l'Impératrice Matilda. Encore à Oxford, Simon de Montfort tint son « Parlement fou » et on prononça le premier édit royal écrit en langue anglaise.

Durant le règne de la catholique Marie Tudor (1553–58), Oxford vit le martyre et la mort sur le bûcher de l'ancien archevêque protestant de Canterbury, Thomas Cranmer, co-auteur d'un célèbre missel anglican, le Book of Common Prayer. Pendant la guerre civile (1642–47) Charles Ier se réfugia un temps à Oxford. Il échappa néanmoins aux parlementaires venus assiéger la ville.

🇩🇪 Man sagt, daß „Oxford so schön ist, weil es auf kleinstem Raum viele seiner architektonisch perfekten historischen Gebäude beherbergt." Oxford ist Englands älteste Universität. Dafür gibt es geographische und historische Gründe. Im frühen Mittelalter waren die Flüsse die Hauptverkehrswege und die Themse war Südenglands Hauptverkehrsader. Man war noch nicht weit beim Brückenbau fortgeschritten und bei Oxford konnten Menschen und Ochsen bei Hinksey durch das seichte Wasser waten. Dieser Furt lag an der südwestlichen Ecke eines von der Themse und der Cherwell gebildeten Ländervierecks. Dieses Viereck, von drei Seiten von Wasser umgeben, steigt von den Flüssen her

etwas an und bildet so eine von Überflutungen sichere, leicht zu verteidigende Lage. König Alfred befestigte es in seinem Kampf gegen die dänischen Eindringlinge. Die angelsächsische Chronik berichtet, daß König Edward es im Jahre 912 für Verteidigungszwecke in Besitz nahm. Über den Fluß Cherwell wurde eine einfache Brücke geschlagen. Heute ist es Magdalen Bridge. Die Straße, die von Osten über die Brücke ging, kreuzle sich mit der Straße von Northampton und dem Norden und lief über den Ochsenfurt (Oxenford) auf dem Weg nach Abingdon und zum Süden an den Quatre Voies, den vier Wegen. So ist es noch heute, nur sind die frühgeschichtlichen Pfade städtische Durchfahrtsstraßen und der Name „Quatre Voies" ist zu „Carfax" geworden.

Seine geographische Lage in der Mitte Südenglands machte Oxford zu ʿeinem bedeutenden Handelszentrum im angelsächsischen England. Hier bot sich auch eine gute Lage für den Bau einer normannischen Burg an. Robert d'Oili erbaute den Turm in 1071 und befestigte den Burggraben von Oxford Castle. Aus vornormannischer Zeit steht nur noch der Turm von St. Michael-at-the-Northgate. Es gibt noch einige normannische Gebäude, wie das Südportal der späteren, gotischen Kirche St. Peter-in-the-East, heute eine Bücherei eines der Kollegien, St. Edmund Hall und Christ Church Kathedrale.

Nach der normannischen Eroberung ergab sich bald eine enge Bindung zwischen Oxford und den englischen Königen. Einige Kilometer von Oxford lag der Wychwoodforst, der das bevorzugte Jagdgebiet der normannischen und angevinischen Könige wurde. Heinrich I. erbaute ein Jagdschloß in Woodstock. Er erbaute auch Beaumont Palast nahe dem heutigen Worcester College, wo sein Großenkel, Richard Löwenherz, geboren wurde. Hier in Oxford belagerte König Stephen im Jahre 1141 die Kaiserin Matilda. Hier in Oxford traf sich das „verrückte Parlament" Simon de Montforts, und hier wurde die erste königliche Proklamation in englischer Sprache ausgegeben. Hier in Oxford wurden Thomas Cranmer und die Bischöfe Latimer und Ridley zu Märtyrern. Während des Bürgerkrieges im 17. Jh. wurde Oxford für einige Zeit König Karls I. Hauptquartier.

Above: Carfax; below: the Martyrs' Memorial, designed by George Gilbert Scott and erected in 1841, commemorates Latimer, Ridley and Cranmer, burnt at the stake in 1555–6.
Ci-dessus: Carfax; ci-dessous: le monument aux martyrs, de George Gilbert Scott (1841) à la mémoire de Latimer, Ridley et Cranmer morts au bûcher en 1555–6.
Oben: Carfax; unten: Märtyrerdenkmal von George Gilbert Scott entworfen und 1841 errichtet für Latimer, Ridley und Cranmer, die 1555 und 1556 den Feuertod erlitten.

Town and Gown

Oxford was a town of tradesmen, whose activities were governed by the merchant guild, and the royal charter, given by Henry II in 1155, guaranteed to it the same privileges as were enjoyed by the citizens of London. But within a few years what might be called another guild, the guild of learning, appeared in Oxford and, winning royal and ecclesiastical favour, began to acquire powers and privileges, which relegated the townspeople to a position of municipal servitude. Without the University Oxford would never have been more than a market town and visitors would not now come to it from all over the world, but its citizens paid a large price in their subservient status, and animosity between Town and Gown continued until recent years.

The medieval university was not a place but a community of Masters of Arts and, just as a boy learned a trade or craft by being apprenticed to a master of his chosen skill and being later accepted as a member of the guild, so a student attended the lectures of the Masters of Arts and after five years of residence, if he was judged worthy, he 'determined', as the word was, and became a Bachelor of Arts. After three more years of residence he 'incepted', becoming a Master of Arts with a degree, which was a licence to teach, granted by an ecclesiastical authority, and was admitted as a voting Member of the University.

Education in the Middle Ages was in the hands of the Church and from early years there had been teachers of good repute in many English towns such as Winchester, York and Canterbury. English scholars had lectured on the continent of Europe, but there was no centre of learning in England of the standard of a university. Oxford's saint, St Frideswide, a Saxon lady who died in 735, founded a religious house which gained a reputation for learning, which it shared with the college of canons of the collegiate church of St George in Robert D'Oili's castle. Other scholarly clerics gathered at Oxford, which became a centre of scholarship easily accessible for students in the southern half of England. By the middle of the twelfth century its reputation extended across the sea to Paris, whose University attracted scholars from all over western Europe and to which English students were accustomed to go, when they could, to pursue their higher studies. In 1167 all this came to a sudden end. The King of France expelled all foreign scholars and Henry II forbad English students to go to Paris, whether the French king was willing to have them or not. Its convenient situation, its reputation and its particular relationship with the Univeristy of Paris made Oxford the obvious alternative and by 1170 it became a place at which a sufficient number of subjects were being taught at a sufficiently high level to be called a *Studium Generale*: that is, a university.

The effect of this sudden influx of teachers and students into Oxford was horrendous. Today one of

William of Wykeham (seated centre top) holds New College Chapel and Hall, and (top left) Archbishop Chichele holds the Chapel of All Souls College (MS New College 288, fols. 3ᵛ–4) (by courtesy of the Warden and Fellows of New College, Oxford).
William de Wykeham (assis, en haut au centre), New College Chapel et Hall et (en haut à gauche) l'archevêque Chichele, chapelle de All Souls College.
William of Wykeham (oben Mitte) hält New College Chapel und Hall, und (oben links) Erzbischof Chichele die Kapelle von All Souls College haltend.

Oxford's problems is to find accommodation for the great number of students at the University, the colleges of further education and the English language schools, which have settled in the city, but in 1167 the problem was even greater. It was a town with only some 4,000 or 5,000 inhabitants and suddenly something like 1,500 people arrived and required lodging, food and all the other needs of a student population. They were an undisciplined collection of scholars, given to excessive drinking and consequent brawls among themselves, not averse from stealing and frequently involved in fights with the people of the town, who on their side saw in the usually poor scholars an opportunity of making money by charging exorbitant rents for accommodation and giving short measure in the markets, from which the students had to buy their food, their ink and parchment and their other requirements. In 1209 there was a conflict of unusual ferocity, a student killed a townswoman, the townspeople in reprisal hanged two completely innocent members of the University and many of the teachers and students fled from Oxford. Some went to Cambridge, where a considerable amount of academic activity was being practised. As with Oxford in 1167, so in 1209 the influx of teachers and students fleeing from another community enabled Cambridge to become a *Studium Generale* or university.

At Oxford the University was under the jurisdiction of the Bishop of Lincoln, in whose diocese it was. The deplorable situation was examined by the Church and a Papal Charter regulating the affairs of the University was issued in 1214. The Norman and Angevin kings were great patrons of learning and their ties with the town of Oxford brought them into contact with the young University to which they transferred their favour. Ecclesiastical and royal regulations gave the Chancellor, the local representative of the Bishop, increasing authority over the citizens. In 1229 another migration of scholars from Paris caused further problems of lodging and marketing and a climax was reached on St Scholastica's Day, 10 February 1355. For two days chaos reigned. The townspeople, reinforced by 2,000 country folk, became a mob which broke into students' halls and lodgings, destroying their books and other belongings. The scholars retaliated with bows and arrows, but the townsfolk were too numerous and almost all the academic population fled from Oxford. The Bishop lost no time in laying the town under an Interdict and for a year no masses could be said and even funerals could not be conducted by a priest. When the Interdict was lifted, the Bishop imposed a humiliating penance on the town. Every year on St Scholastica's Day the Mayor and Bailiffs and sixty citizens had to go to the University Church of St Mary the Virgin to attend a mass offered at their expense for the souls of the sixty scholars killed in the riot. This annual penance continued till 1825. After the riot, control of the market was given by royal decree to the Chancellor, whose officers were empowered to test the weights and measures and quality of food and drink sold by the traders, and it was not till 1889 that control of the market was restored to the city. A new charter given to the University in 1355 also gave the Chancellor power to punish breaches of the peace committed by laymen even if no member of the University was involved. An offshoot of this survived till 1968 when Parliamentary legislation deprived the Vice-Chancellor, who had become the administrative head of the University, of the right to try certain civil cases involving an undergraduate, if he cared to call the case from the ordinary magistrates' courts to his own court. Not unnaturally much tact and conscious effort have been needed during the last hundred years to create friendly relations between Town and Gown.

🇫🇷 Oxford était à l'origine placée sous la double autorité de la guilde des marchands et d'une charte royale octroyée par Henri II en 1155. Quelques années plus tard, cependant, une nouvelle « guilde », celle du savoir, gagna rapidement les faveurs de la cour et du clergé, reléguant les citoyens d'Oxford à un rang subalterne. Ceux-ci payaient cher la célébrité que leur apportait l'université et un fort antagonisme se fit jour.

Malgré la présence de professeurs renommés dans quelques grandes villes, l'Angleterre ne possédait pas alors d'université à proprement parler. Grace à la présence de quelques ecclésiastiques érudits, Oxford commença à attirer de nom-

breux étudiants de toute l'Angleterre du Sud. Un plus grand nombre cependant continuait à se rendre à la Sorbonne, jusqu'en 1167, date à laquelle Louis VII le jeune interdit celle-ci aux étudiants étrangers. Cette décision donna un coup de fouet inattendu à Oxford qui dès 1170 avait accru le nombre de sujets enseignés ainsi que le niveau de son enseignement suffisamment pour recevoir le titre de *Studium Generale* (université). La décision du roi de France fit donc affluer à Oxford, qui comptait alors environ 5.000 habitants, plus de 1.500 étudiants qu'il fallait loger et nourrir et qui, de plus, étaient indisciplinés et enclins aux excès de boisson et bagarres, voire au vol. De leur côté, les citoyens d'Ox-

ford virent dans les étudiants une source d'argent facile et réclamèrent des prix exorbitants pour leurs chambres et nourriture. Les troubles culminèrent en 1209: un étudiant tua un des habitants de la ville; ceux-ci se vengèrent en pendant deux étudiants innocents. Professeurs et étudiants partirent en masse pour Cambridge qui grâce à cet apport prit à son tour

le titre d'université.

Une charte papale de 1214 tenta de rétablir l'ordre à Oxford. Grâce à celle-ci et à l'attitude favorable des souverains, l'université accrut considérablement son emprise sur la ville. Le 10 février 1355 pourtant un vent de folie souffla à nouveau sur la ville. Pendant deux jours, les citoyens d'Oxford, avec des renforts venus des environs, envahirent les logements et salles de cours des étudiants, détruisant tout sur leur passage. Les étudiants leur répondirent avec des arcs et des flèches mais, étant plus faibles en nombre, ils durent s'enfuir en compagnie de leurs professeurs. En punition, l'évêque fit interdire les messes et enterrements à Oxford pendant un

The courtyard of the Golden Cross Inn, Cornmarket, in the nineteenth century, by John Buckler (Bodl. MS Don. a. 2 (26)).
La cour de Golden Cross Inn, Corn-

market, au 19ᵉ siècle, par John Buckler.
Der Hof des Gasthauses zum Goldenen Kreuz, Cornmarket, im 19. Jh. von John Buckler.

an, à la suite de quoi, tous les ans, le jour anniversaire des émeutes, le maire, les baillis et soixante citoyens durent se rendre dans l'église St-Mary-the-Virgin assister à une messe (dite à leurs frais) pour le repos des âmes des soixante victimes étudiants et universitaires. Cette coutume dura jusqu'en 1825. De même, après les émeutes, la permission fut donnée au

Overleaf: *Turl Street – 'the Turl' – painted by J. M. W. Turner (1775–1851)* ▶
(by courtesy of the Ashmolean Museum, Oxford).
Au verso: *Turl Street – « The Turl » par J. M. W. Turner (1775–1851).*
Umseitig: *Turlstraße – „the Turl" – von J. M. W. Turner gemalt (1775–1851).*

Chancellor de l'université de con-
trôler les poids et mesures utilisés et
la qualité des produits sur le marché
d'Oxford, coutume en vigueur jusqu'en 1889. Enfin, une nouvelle
charte de 1355 donnait au Chancellor
des pouvoirs judiciaires sur les citoyens d'Oxford, pouvoirs qui ne
furent abolis qu'en 1968. On ne
s'étonnera pas, avec un tel passé,
qu'il ait fallu énormément de tact et
de bonne volonté pour créer des
rapports cordiaux durables entre la
ville et l'université.

Oxford war eine Handels-
stadt, die von den Zünften
beherrscht wurde. Es kam eine
weitere Zunft hinzu, die „Zunft der
Gelehrsamkeit". Sie gewann bald die
Gunst des Königs und der Geistlich-
keit und damit Macht und
Privilegien. Ohne seine Universität
wäre Oxford ein Marktflecken geblieben, aber seine Bürger wurden
durch sie in eine untergeordnete
Stellung verdrängt und die Ab-
neigung zwischen Stadt und Universität blieb bis zur jüngsten Zeit
bestehen.

Die mittelalterliche Universität
war eine Gemeinschaft von Magistern. Ein Student, der die Vorlesun-
gen seiner Magister besuchte, wurde
nach fünf Jahren dortigen Wohnens
„bestimmt" (wie man es nannte) und
Bakkalaureus. Nach weiteren drei
Jahren wurde er „aufgenommen",
das hieß er promovierte zum Magister. Nun hatte er die von einer
kirchlichen Autorität gewährte
Lehrqualifikation und wurde Mit-
glied der Universität mit Wahl-
berechtigung.

Die Erziehung lag im Mittelalter
in den Händen der Kirche. In vielen
englischen Städten wie Winchester,
York und Canterbury gab es schon
in früher Zeit ausgezeichnete Lehrer.
Englische Gelehrte hielten wohl Vor-
lesungen in Europa, aber es gab in
England kein Lehrzentrum, das dem
Niveau einer Universität gleichkam.
Oxfords Schutzpatronin, die heilige
Frideswide, eine sächsische Dame,
die 735 starb, gründete ein religiöses
Haus, das sich einen Namen für
seine Gelehrsamkeit machte. Eine
ähnliche Reputation genoß das Stif-
terkolleg der Kollegiatskirche St.
George in Robert d'Oilis Burg.
Andere geistliche Gelehrte siedelten
sich in Oxford an, das so bald zu
einem Zentrum der Gelehrsamkeit
wurde. Mitte des 12. Jh. hatte sich
sein Ruf bis nach Paris verbreitet,
dessen Universität Gelehrte aus ganz

*Left: the covered market in 1909, still
in existence and almost unaltered
today (by courtesy of Oxfordshire
County Libraries); above: Radcliffe
Square with All Souls College in the
background, painted by Thomas
Rowlandson (?1756–1827) (by courtesy of the Ashmolean Museum,
Oxford); below: Town and Gown
come to blows on Guy Fawkes Night
(Bodl. Manning 8° 147).*
*A gauche: le marché couvert en 1909
aujourd'hui presque intact; ci-dessus:*
Radcliffe Square avec, au fond, All
Souls College par Thomas Rowlandson (?1756–1827); ci-dessous: la ville
et l'université s'affrontent pendant la
nuit de Guy Fawkes.
*Links: Markthallen um 1909, die
heute noch unverändert stehen; oben:
der Radcliffe Platz mit All Souls
College im Hintergrund von Thomas
Rowlandson gemalt (?1756–1827);
unten: Stadt- und Universitätsmit-
glieder geraten sich zur Guy Fawkes
Nacht in die Haare.*

Westeuropa anzog, sowie englische
Studenten für höhere Studien. All
das endete im Jahr 1167. Der fran-
zösische König verwies alle aus-
ländischen Gelehrten des Landes
und der englische König Heinrich II.
verbot englischen Studenten in Paris
zu studieren. So wurde Oxford –
bedingt durch seine günstige Lage im
südlichen England, seinen schon
etablierten Ruf und seine bisherigen
Beziehungen zur Universität von
Paris – zum Sitz der Gelehrsamkeit
erwählt. Das Niveau der mannig-
fachen Fächer, die um 1170 ange-
boten wurden, war hoch, sodaß man
durchaus schon von einem Studium
Generale sprechen konnte, was mit
einer Universität gleichwertig ist.

Die Folgen des Zustroms von
Lehrern und Schülern nach Oxford
waren immens. Oxford war dann ein
kleines Städtchen von 4.000 bis 5.000
Einwohnern, denen sich plötzlich
1.500 Leute zugesellten. Im Jahre
1209 kam es zu einem heftigen
Konflikt, nachdem ein Student eine
Frau umgebracht hatte. Die Städter
rächten sich mit dem Erhängen
zweier, völlig unschuldiger Univer-
sitätsmitglieder. Viele Lehrer und

Studenten flohen daraufhin von Oxford. Einige gingen nach Cambridge, wo schon beträchtliche akademische Aktivität herrschte.

Im Jahre 1229 verursachte ein weiterer Zustrom von Pariser Gelehrten erneute Unterkunftsprobleme. Am St. Scholasticatag, am 10. Februar 1355 kam es zu schweren Unruhen. Zwei Tage lang herrschte Chaos. Die Städter, unterstützt von etwa 2.000 Landbewohnern, brachen in die Quartiere der Studenten ein und zerstörten deren Bücher und persönliche Habe. Die Studenten verteidigten sich, waren aber der zahlenmäßigen Überlegenheit der Bürger nicht gewachsen. Fast die gesamte akademische Bevölkerung floh. Der Bischof tat die Stadt in Acht und Bann. Nach Aufhebung des Bannes erlegte der Bischof der Stadt eine demütigende Strafe auf. Alljährlich am St. Scholasticatag mußten Bürgermeister, Amtmänner und 60 Bürger in der Universitätskirche von St.-Mary-the-Virgin an einer Messe teilnehmen (deren Kosten sie trugen), die für das Seelenheil der in dem Aufruhr umgekommenen 60 Gelehrten gehalten wurde. Diese jährliche Buße fand bis 1825 statt. Während der letzten 150 Jahre hat es verständlicherweise des größten Taktes und bewußter Anstrengungen bedurft, um ein gutes Einvernehmen zwischen Stadt und Universität zu schaffen.

Top: St Aldates before the demolition of houses on the right-hand side to create Christ Church Memorial Garden; middle: Cornmarket bedecked with flags for the coronation of Edward VII and Queen Alexandra in 1902; bottom: horse-trams in High Street – 'the High' – outside All Souls (all three pictures by courtesy of Oxfordshire County Libraries).
En haut: St Aldates avant la démolition des maisons à droite pour faire place à un jardin; au milieu: Cornmarket pavoisé pour le couronnement d'Edouard VII en 1902; en bas: tramways tirés par des chevaux dans la High Street (« the High ») devant All Souls.
Oben: St. Aldates vor Abbruch der Häuser auf der rechten Seite, um den Christ Church Memorial Garten anzulegen; Mitte: Flaggengeschmückter Cornmarket anläßlich der Krönung Edwards VII. und Königins Alexandra im Jahre 1902; unten: Pferdebahn in der High Street – „the High" genannt – vor All Souls.

The Colleges & University

When by 1170 the University of Oxford became a reality, it was a reality without any building of which it could be said, 'This is the University'. The community of the Masters of Arts had no premises and each Master had himself to rent a room from a citizen of the town in which to lecture. Nor did the University have any accommodation for teachers or scholars, who had to find what lodgings they could. The situation was eased to some extent by graduates who rented houses to provide lodging for a number of scholars. These houses were called halls and the graduate in charge was the Principal; but in general the lives of the scholars were squalid and hard and their behaviour did not endear them to the townsfolk. In 1249 a bequest was made to the University for the maintenance of scholars and it was decided to create a little community of Masters, together with others who cared to live with them, in a hall. The University bought some houses scattered around St Mary's church, one of which they called the University's Hall, in which teachers and scholars could live together. (This first establishment became University College later on.) The numbers concerned were small, but the idea was far-reaching. A year or two before 1270 John de Balliol, a rich baron of Barnard Castle in the north of England and husband of Devorguilla, a Scottish princess, gave money to endow a house for scholars in Oxford and a little community was established. It comprised sixteen students or, as we should say today, undergraduates, whose funds were administered for them by the Proctors. Neither of these two earliest foundations was a college, but they did embody the new principle shown in the University's Hall: Masters and scholars lived in the same building and it was hoped that this would improve the morals as well as the living conditions of the students. An Oxford or Cambridge college is a self-governing community, 'a corporate fraternity, with a common life, common property, a common Head'. The first real college to be established was created by Walter de Merton. He was a great

prelate, from 1261 to 1263 Chancellor of England and later Bishop of Rochester. He obtained authority to assign two manors to the Priory of Merton for the support of clerics engaged in academic study. In 1264 he established 'the House of the Scholars of Merton' at Merton in Surrey for the perpetual support of twenty scholars at Oxford and began the building of Merton College. He compiled detailed Statutes, which were for long the model for collegiate foundations at both Oxford and Cambridge. In 1284 Peterhouse was founded in Cambridge with statutes based on those of Merton, and in the fourteenth century in both Oxford and Cambridge other colleges were founded on the same model. The fourteenth-century Mob Quad at Merton is the oldest quadrangle or

'Sending-down' was the most severe punishment for persistent laziness or bad behaviour – it meant the end of an undergraduate's University career (by courtesy of Oxfordshire County Libraries).
Le renvoi définitif pour paresse ou mauvaise conduite était la plus sévère punition, signifiant la fin d'une carrière universitaire.
,,Relegieren" war die härteste Strafe für faule Studenten oder solche mit schlechtem Benehmen und bedeutete das Ende des Universitätsbesuches.

court in either Oxford or Cambridge. Its library has been in use for over 600 years and the great collection of late thirteenth- and early fourteenth-century stained glass in the chapel is outstanding.

Exeter, Oriel, Queen's and other colleges were founded in the fourteenth century and then in 1379 William of Wykeham, the Bishop of Winchester, began the building of

New College, a much larger project than anything planned before. It was to have seventy scholars over the age of fifteen, and a few years later he founded Winchester College as a school to provide young men of a high standard to be scholars of his college in Oxford. The plan of quadrangle, chapel, library, dining hall and staircases with rooms for teachers and scholars, begun at Merton, was carried out on a larger scale at New College with the addition of a cloister. The founders wanted to build it right up against the wall of the town and royal permission for this was given only on the undertaking that the college would be responsible for the upkeep of the defences. Not many years ago the Warden gave a garden party for the Mayor and City Council and

provided scaling ladders which he invited them to climb in order to see whether this undertaking was being honoured or whether the conditions of the twentieth century made it no longer necessary.

During the next three centuries the building of colleges went on. The original idea was that a college should be a community of teachers and young men who had already

become Bachelors of Arts, not of teachers and undergraduates. New College was founded, however, to take scholars straight from school, and when William of Waynflete founded Magdalen, in 1448, there was another innovation. In addition to forty Fellows and thirty scholars there were to be independent students paying for themselves – the forerunners of the 'commoners' of later days. All Souls, founded in 1438 by Archbishop Chichele, alone maintained the graduate principle. It continued to admit only those who had taken their Bachelor's degree and were maintained by the college as Fellows.

In 1525 Cardinal Wolsey was given permission by the Pope to dissolve the Augustinian Priory of St Frideswide and he used the funds acquired from this and the dissolution of twenty-two small monastic houses to build a college, called Cardinal College. He fell from power before he finished it and King Henry VIII founded first a small establishment in its place and then in 1546, with the ecclesiastical wealth placed at his disposal by the Reformation, he refounded it as Christ Church, a unique foundation comprising both the Cathedral Chapter of the new diocese of Oxford, carved out of the earlier vast diocese of Lincoln, and a college. The Dean of the Cathedral is head of the college and the canons of the Chapter are members of the Governing Body of the college. Wolsey intended to demolish the Priory church and build a great chapel like, but larger than, the chapel of King's College at Cambridge; but in the meantime he would use the church as his college chapel. Henry VIII decided that, at any rate for the time being, this church could be the cathedral of the new diocese: and so it has remained ever since. The beautiful twelfth-century church has thus been saved from destruction.

The building of the new colleges continued in the sixteenth and seventeenth centuries and additions to existing colleges such as Peckwater Quadrangle at Christ Church in the early eighteenth century, and the building of Keble College in the nineteenth, continued academic building, up to the middle of the twentieth century when a new need arose. Whereas in the past a first degree, the degree of Bachelor of Arts, was all that was required for most purposes, a second degree, such as a Doctorate of Philosophy, began to be demanded by the employment market and so the number of graduate students, formerly very small, greatly increased. Every college began to accept graduate students, but new colleges were founded for Fellows and graduate students only, some of them scholars but most paying fees. Nuffield, St Antony's, Wolfson and Green Colleges were built to meet this need and St Catherine's was built for both undergraduates and post-graduate students.

During the last hundred years there has been another development. During all previous centuries only men came to the University, but in the second half of the nineteenth century women began to say that they too should be able to have a university education and in 1878 Lady Margaret Hall was founded as the first women's college, followed by Somerville, St Hilda's, St Hugh's and St Anne's. Their students could attend lectures and take university examinations, but they were awarded only diplomas, not degrees. This discrimination was abolished in 1920 and · more recently men's colleges began to admit women as undergraduates and women's colleges to admit men. Now almost every college is open to both men and women.

It was not till the fourteenth century, when a small Congregation House was built beside St Mary's church, that the University began to own property. A century later a University library came into being. In 1444 Humfrey Duke of Gloucester, brother of King Henry IV, gave a collection of manuscript books to the University and built a magnificent library with a lecture hall beneath it. At the beginning of the seventeenth century Sir Thomas Bodley became librarian and built a quadrangle attached to Duke Humfrey's library, the whole being called the Bodleian Library. In 1749 the architect, James Gibbs, was commissioned to add extra reading rooms and storage space and built the Radcliffe Camera, and in 1946 a large new building was opened on the other side of Broad Street. All these buildings and specialist libraries and the ever-increasing number of laboratories required for scientific research and study are owned by the University, whose property shows the architecture of every age from the fourteenth century to the present time.

Opposite page, top: New College showing the seventeenth- and early eighteenth-century Garden Quad; ***middle:*** *Keble College, designed by William Butterfield in 1868;* ***bottom:*** *Lady Margaret Hall, founded in the late nineteenth century.* ***This page:*** *a view of the High looking west towards Carfax – Queen's College is centre, right, and the Examination Schools are centre, left.*
Page opposée, en haut: *New College, avec le Garden Quad (17ᵉ et début 18ᵉ siècles);* ***au centre:*** *Keble College, œuvre de William Butterfield en 1868;* ***en bas:*** *Lady Margaret Hall, fondé fin*

19ᵉ siècle. ***Sur cette page:*** *vue de « The High » vers l'Ouest, en direction de Carfax – Queen's College est au centre, à droite et les centres d'examens sont au centre, à gauche.*
Gegenüberliegende Seite, oben: *New College mit seinem aus dem 17. und frühen 18. Jh. stammenden Gartenhof;* ***Mitte:*** *Keble College 1868 von William Butterfield entworfen;* ***unten:*** *Lady Margaret Hall wurde Ende des 19. Jh. gegründet.* ***Diese Seite:*** *Blick von der High Street westlich auf Carfax – Queen's College liegt Mitte rechts, die Prüfungsschulen liegen Mitte links.*

Right: the Old Quadrangle (1509) of Brasenose College, with the dome of the Radcliffe Camera and the spire of the University Church, St Mary's, beyond, by J. M. W. Turner. Brasenose was founded by Sir Richard Sutton and the Bishop of Lincoln in 1509. It was built on the site of two former halls, Brasenose Hall and Little University Hall; the name 'Brasenose' probably came from the form of its medieval door-knocker. The handsome Gate Tower was built in 1512. The Cloister, Library and Chapel are seventeenth century, the Chapel having fine fan vaulting. The scene shown in this painting has hardly altered today; **below:** Colonel James Boden, an Oxford resident at the beginning of the nineteenth century, by Thomas Rowlandson (both pictures by courtesy of the Ashmolean Museum, Oxford).

*A **droite:** le Old Quadrangle (1509) de Brasenose College, avec le dôme de la Radcliffe Camera et le clocher de St Mary's, église de l'université, par J. M. W. Turner; **ci-dessous:** le colonel James Boden, membre d'Oxford au début du 19ᵉ siècle, par Thomas Rowlandson.*

Rechts: Old Quadrangle (1509) von Brasenose College mit Kuppel der Radcliffe Camera und dem Turm der Universitätskirche von St. Mary im Hintergrund nach einem Gemälde von J. M. W. Turner; **unten:** Colonel James Boden, ein Oxforder Bürger des frühen 19. Jh. von Thomas Rowlandson.

Above: the Radcliffe Camera, part of the Bodleian Library; ***below left:*** these four plates show the gowns worn in the eighteenth and nineteenth centuries by ***(left to right)*** a Scholar, a Nobleman, a Commoner and a Gentleman Commoner – today, undergraduates wear gowns with long sleeves if they are Scholars or Exhibitioners (holding awards) and sleeveless short gowns with bands behind if they are Commoners (by courtesy of Oxfordshire County Libraries).

Ci-dessus: la Radcliffe Camera qui fait partie de la bibliothèque Bodleian; ***ci-dessous à gauche:*** ces quatre gravures montrent les toges portées au 18e et 19e siècles par ***(de gauche à droite)*** un scholar, un nobleman, un commoner et un gentleman commoner (différents types d'étudiants selon leur type de bourse). De nos jours les étudiants ayant une bourse spéciale portent une toge à manches longues et les étudiants ayant une bourse ordinaire portent une toge courte sans manches.

Oben: die Radcliffe Camera sind Teil der Bodleian Bücherei; ***links unten:*** die vier Drucke zeigen die Gewänder, wie man sie im 18. und 19. Jh. .an der Universität trug. ***Von links nach rechts:*** ein Scholar, ein Adliger, ein Commoner und ein Gentleman Commoner. Heute tragen immatrikulierte Studenten langärmelige Gewänder, wenn sie Scholars sind und kurzärmelige Überwürfe mit Bändern, wenn sie Commoners sind.

Lavish entertaining in College rooms, a common practice before the Second World War, is now almost unknown (by courtesy of Oxfordshire County Libraries).

Il était courant avant-guerre, pour les étudiants de mener la grande vie dans leurs résidences, pratique maintenant presque disparue.
Üppige Gelage in den Kollegzimmern vor dem 2. Weltkrieg an der Tagesordnung sind heute fast unbekannt.

sity's Hall (devenu University College) abrita la première communauté
de ce genre. Vers 1270, un riche
baron nommé John de Balliol
finança une autre entreprise de ce
type, comprenant seize étudiants.
Aucun de ces deux établissements
n'était un collège à proprement
parler, mais ils incarnaient le prin-
cipe même du collège, à savoir un
groupe de maîtres et de chercheurs
boursiers vivant sous le même toit.
Le premier véritable collège fut créé
par Walter de Merton. Ce grand
prélat fit édifier Merton College en
1264, le dotant de statuts détaillés
qui devaient longtemps servir de
modèle aux autres collèges d'Oxford
et de Cambridge. A Merton College
on peut encore de nos jours admirer
Mob Quad, la plus ancienne cour
(*quadrangle*) d'Oxford ou de Cambridge, ainsi que la bibliothèque (en
service depuis plus de 600 ans) et une
merveilleuse collection de vitraux du
XIVe siècle dans la chapelle.

Exeter, Oriel, Queen's et d'autres
suivirent au XIVe siècle. En 1379
William de Wykeham, évêque de
Winchester, commença la construction de New College, entreprise
d'une plus grande envergure que les
précédentes. New College devait en
effet abriter soixante-dix étudiants et
chercheurs et quelques années plus
tard Wykeham fonda l'école de
Winchester destinée à former les
futurs étudiants de son collège
d'Oxford. New College, avec sa
cour, sa chapelle, bibliothèque,
réfectoire et chambres pour maîtres
et étudiants, suivait en plus vaste
le plan de base de Merton avec
l'adjonction d'un cloître. New College innovait également en matière

L'université d'Oxford à sa
naissance en 1170 était à la
rue. Les maîtres ne possédaient pas
de locaux et faisaient leurs cours
dans des chambres meublées. Les
étudiants, de même, devaient trouver
leur propre logement. Certains com-
mencèrent à louer des maisons
nommées *halls*, à la tête desquelles
était placé un proviseur (*Principal*).
Les conditions d'existence dans ces

établissements étaient cependant
peu satisfaisantes et en 1249 une
demande fut faite à l'université pour
le soutien financier de ses membres;
il fut décidé de créer une petite
communauté de maîtres et chercheurs, groupés dans un *hall*, aux
frais de l'université. Cette dernière
acquit quelques maisons situées
autour de l'église St Mary's et l'une
d'entre elles, baptisée the Univer-

d'étudiants car outre les chercheurs, il acceptait des jeunes gens sortis tout droit de l'école. Magdalen College, fondé en 1448, inaugura l'arrivée d'étudiants sans bourse de l'université, nommés plus tard *commoners*, par rapport aux boursiers (*scholars*). Seul le collège All Souls, fondé en 1438, maintient encore l'esprit original du collège composé uniquement de chercheurs.

En 1525 le cardinal Wolsey profita de fonds acquis grâce à la dissolution de monastères pour édifier un collège, sous le nom de Cardinal's College. Wolsey fut disgrâcié avant d'avoir pu le terminer mais le roi Henri VIII le fit ouvrir et plus tard, avec des fonds apportés par la Réforme, le fit agrandir et rebaptiser Christ Church. Christ Church était un établissement unique groupant le Chapitre de la cathédrale du diocèse d'Oxford et un collège; le doyen de la cathédrale était en même temps à la tête du collège. Henri VIII fit alors des plans pour la reconstruction de l'église, désirant surpasser la chapelle de King's College à Cambridge. Ces plans ne furent jamais menés à bien et il fut décidé de conserver l'église en place (XIIe

siècle) et d'en faire temporairement la cathédrale du nouveau diocèse – ce qu'elle est restée jusqu'à nos jours.

Au cours des siècles, la construction de nouveaux collèges ainsi que l'agrandissement des anciens s'est poursuivie au fur et à mesure que le nombre d'étudiants et de chercheurs augmentait et que de nouveaux besoins se faisaient sentir. Nuffield, St Antony's, Wolfson et Green Colleges furent fondés pour accueillir uniquement les étudiants préparant des doctorats.

La reconnaissance du droit des femmes à l'éducation supérieure vers le milieu du XIXe siècle changea également la physionomie d'Oxford (jusqu'alors bastion masculin). Lady Margaret Hall, fondé en 1878, fut le premier collège féminin et fut suivi de Somerville, St Hilda's, St Hugh's et St Anne's. La plupart des collèges sont maintenant mixtes.

Il faut enfin mentionner la célèbre bibliothèque d'Oxford, the Bodleian Library, du nom de Sir Thomas Bodley, bibliothécaire du début du XVIIe siècle, qui ajouta une cour à l'établissement fondé en 1444. La bibliothèque a été constamment agrandie depuis.

Als 1170 die Universität von Oxford Wirklichkeit wurde, war es eine Wirklichkeit ohne jede Gebäude, auf die man hätte zeigen können und sagen: „Das ist die Universität." Der Gemeinschaft der Magister standen keine Räume zur Verfügung. Jeder Magister mußte sich von einem Bürger einen Raum mieten, in dem er lehren konnte. Einige Lehrer mieteten Häuser, um Unterkünfte für Studenten zu haben. In diesen Häusern war der Promovierte, „Principal" genannt, verantwortlich. In 1249 wurde eine kleine Gemeinschaft von Magistern geschaffen, die in einem großen Haus zusammenlebte. Die Universität kaufte einige Häuser um St. Mary's Kirche auf. Eines davon wurde „University's Hall" genannt. Hier konnten Lehrer und Schüler wohnen. (Dieses Gebäude wurde später „University College".) Die Zahl der dort Lebenden war klein, aber die Idee trug Früchte. Um 1270 spendete John de Balliol, ein reicher Baron, Geld für ein Studentenhaus. Die kleine Gemeinschaft bestand aus 16 Studenten. Keine dieser ersten Gründungen war ein Kolleg, aber es zeigte sich hier schon das neue

Prinzip: Lehrer und Studenten lebten im gleichen Gebäude zusammen und man hoffte, daß das sich auf Moral und Lebensweise der Studenten auswirkte. Ein Oxford oder Cambridge Kolleg ist eine sich selbstregierende Gemeinschaft, „eine korporative Verbindung mit Gemeinschaftsleben, gemeinsamem Eigentum, einem gemeinsamen Leiter". Das erste Kolleg dieser Art stammt von Walter de Merton. Er war ein großer Prälat, von 1261 bis 1263 Kanzler von England und Bischof von Rochester. Er erhielt die Erlaubnis, zwei große Gutshäuser der Priorei von Merton zu übertragen, um studierende Theologen zu unterstützen. 1264 gründete er das „Haus der Stipendiaten von Merton" in Merton in Surrey zur dauernden Unterstützung von 20 Stipendiaten in Oxford und fing mit dem Bau von Merton College an. 1284 wurde in Cambridge Peterhouse gegründet mit Statuten, die denen von Merton glichen und im 14. Jh. folgten in Oxford und Cambridge der Bau weiterer Kollegien mit ähnlichen Satzungen.

Exeter, Oriel, Queen's und einige andere Kollegien sind alle Gründungen des 14. Jhs. Der Bau von New College von William Wykeham, Bischof von Winchester im Jahre 1379 begonnen, war auf einer größeren Ebene für 70 Studenten. Einige Jahre später gründete er Winchester College.

Der Bau von Kollegien ging während der nächsten 3 Jahrhunderte weiter. Erst New College, in 1448 Magdalen College und All Souls wurde 1438 von Erzbischof Chichele begründet.

Das von Kardinal Wolsey gegründete Kardinalskolleg wurde nach dessen Sturz von Heinrich VIII. übernommen und neu unter dem Namen Christ Church gegründet, eine einmalige Gründung, die Domkapitel und die neue Diozese von Oxford einbeschloß. Der Dekan der Kathedrale ist Haupt des Kollegs und die Domherren sind Mitglieder der regierenden Kolleggruppe.

Das 16. und 17. Jh. sah Erweiterungen und Neugründungen wie den Peckwater Platz von Christ Church und den Bau von Keble College. Das 20. Jh. brachte eine weitere neue Einrichtung. Bisher hatte die Universitätsprüfung nach Studium gereicht. Jetzt wurde vom Arbeitsmarkt eine 2. Promovierung gewünscht, wie der Dr. phil. Damit erhöhte sich die Zahl der Studieren-

The Upper Library at Christ Church has elaborate plasterwork decorating its ceiling and upper walls, handsome fittings of Norwegian oak, and Venetian windows.

La Grande Bibliothèque (Upper Library) de Christ Church est richement décorée de moulages au plafond et sur les murs, boiseries et fenêtres vénitiennes.

Die obere Bibliothek in Christ Church zeigt feine Stukkaturarbeit an Wänden und Decken, schöne Täfelung aus norwegischer Eiche und venezianische Fenster.

den wieder beträchtlich. Die Kollegien Nuffield, St. Antony's, Wolfson und Green wurden nur für die weiteren Studien bereits promovierter Studenten gebaut. St. Catherine ist für neu immatrikulierte und promovierte Studenten.

In den letzten hundert Jahren sah man in Oxford den Einzug weiblicher Studenten. Lady Margaret Hall, 1878 gegründet, wurde das erste Kolleg für Studentinnen. Es folgten Somerville, St. Hilda's, St. Hugh's und St. Anne. Heute nimmt fast jedes Kolleg Studenten und Studentinnen auf.

Der Herzog von Gloucester gab 1444 eine Sammlung von Manuskripten an die Universität und baute eine großartige Bibliothek mit einem Vorlesungssaal darunter. Im 17. Jh. wurde Sir Thomas Bodley Bibliothekar und vergrößerte den Bau, der sich von nun an Bodleian Bibliothek nannte. Der Architekt James Gibbs fügte 1749 extra Leseräume und die sog. Radcliffe Camera hinzu. 1946 kam ein weiteres großes Gebäude in der Broad Street der Bibliothek gegenüberliegend hinzu. Alle diese Gebäude Sachbüchereien, Laboratorien für Forschung und Studium gehören der Universität.

The Expanding City

It was not until a Royal Commission had issued its Report in 1854 that dons, the University teachers, were allowed to marry. This caused a new housing need, another problem imposed by the University on the town with echoes of the influx of teachers and students in 1167. The main area developed to meet this new need was North Oxford along and radiating from the roads to Banbury and Woodstock. If dons had been allowed to marry a hundred years earlier, North Oxford would have been a second Bath. Instead, it became a red brick suburb of large family houses with gardens, an area of Victorian domestic architecture. A wise requirement was imposed: every garden had to have at least two flowering trees and now North Oxford has a profusion of blossoms in springtime.

Another date with no less far-reaching consequences was 1877 when William Morris was born at Oxford. As a young man he opened a cycle repair shop in the High Street. In 1898 he moved to larger premises at the corner of Holywell and Longwall Streets and opened Morris Garages there. In 1912 he moved to Cowley, four miles east of Oxford, and there established Morris Motors, which, reinforced by Pressed Steel, quickly grew into the giant which has become British Leyland. William Morris, created Lord Nuffield, used his wealth for many charitable purposes and was a great benefactor of the University, but so large an industrial complex so near the city has caused great problems, which environmental planning was too late to avoid. Urban growth has eaten into the countryside all over Britain. In Oxford the need to provide houses for the thousands of factory workers employed at Cowley has made the problem especially intense and much of the immediate surrounding countryside has been urbanised. For a time the area of the medieval town was almost buried under an influx of people coming to shop and by the great quantity of traffic which had to pass through the city. The planning of ring roads and one-way streets has greatly helped to alleviate problems which ought never have been allowed to arise and great vehicle-carriers no longer pass through the ancient streets. But great effort and public enquiries instigated by the colleges and the University were necessary to prevent the planners of roads from easing the congestion caused by traffic at the expense of the University Parks and Christ Church Meadow, which are rural spaces of great beauty open for enjoyment by

Above: *a cartoon referring to Lord Nuffield's gifts to the University.*
Ci-dessus: *un dessin humoristique sur le don de Lord Nuffield à Oxford.*
Oben: *Karikatur über Lord Nuffields Spende an die Universität.*

all from dawn to dusk. Shopping centres built at Cowley and other areas on the outskirts of the city have lessened the need for people to come into the centre to shop, but a large shopping centre has been built close to but outside the area of medieval beauty, meeting the needs of those who do not live near the shopping centres of Cowley and elsewhere.

Although many areas round Oxford have become residential suburbs, the rural beauty of the Thames and the Cherwell have been preserved. A survival from medieval Oxford is Port Meadow, an expanse of 400 acres (including the adjoining Wolvercote Common) along the east side of the Thames. Port Meadow is mentioned in Domesday Book, since when 150 acres have been lost. For many centuries it has been a grazing ground for the animals owned by the citizens, which has been mown only once, when Charles I paid the citizens to mow it to provide fodder for his cavalry. Across the river from Port Meadow the country has been preserved and made part of the green belt. The Cherwell valley also has remained a place of rural beauty, running right into the city and joining the great open spaces of the University Parks and Magdalen and Christ Church Meadow where it flows into the Thames, and the old city is still defended by the Cherwell, not from invading armies but from urban development.

Above: *when University teachers were allowed to marry, older dons were horrified!* (both pictures by courtesy of Oxfordshire County Libraries). ***Ci-dessus:*** *l'autorisation du mariage pour les professeurs fit scandale!* ***Oben:*** *Entsetzen älterer Professoren über ihre verheirateten Kollegen!*

Left, top: *William Morris and friends outside his first garage – Morris was a pioneer in the field of mass-production of cars, the first Morris 'Oxford' being built in 1912;* middle: *the other side of Oxford life – a street in St Ebbe's, then one of the poorest districts, in the 1930s (both pictures by courtesy of Oxfordshire County Libraries);* bottom: *the Morris factory at Cowley between the wars (copyright reserved BL Heritage Ltd).* Below: *Frank Cooper's Oxford Marmalade factory c. 1910 (by courtesy of Oxfordshire County Libraries).*

A gauche, en haut: *William Morris et des amis devant son premier garage;*

au centre: *l'autre côté d'Oxford: une rue dans un quartier pauvre (St Ebbe's) dans les années 30.* **En bas:** *l'usine des automobiles Morris à Cowley entre les deux guerres.* **Ci-dessous:** *la fabrique de la célèbre marmelade d'oranges Frank Cooper vers 1910.*

Links oben: *William Morris und Freunde vor seiner ersten Autowerkstatt;* **Mitte:** *eine Straße in St. Ebbe in den 30er Jahren einer der ärmsten Bezirke, zeigt Oxford von seiner anderen Seite;* **unten:** *die Morrisfabrik in Cowley zwischen den beiden Kriegen.* **Unten:** *Frank Coopers Oxforder Apfelsineenkonfitürefabrik um 1910.*

Ce n'est qu'en 1854 qu'il fut permis aux maîtres de l'université d'Oxford de se marier. Cette décision devait avoir une grande influence sur le développement du paysage urbain. En effet, les besoins en logements soudain accrus amenèrent la construction de nouveaux quartiers principalement au Nord de la ville. Un arrêté stipula que chaque nouvel habitant devait planter deux arbres portant des fleurs dans son jardin et une visite de ces quartiers s'impose au printemps pour admirer la splendeur de ces floraisons.

Une autre date marquante dans l'histoire d'Oxford est celle de la naissance, en 1877, de William Morris. Jeune homme, il ouvrit un atelier de réparations de vélos dans la High Street. Ses activités florissantes le firent déménager au coin de Holywell et Longwall Streets pour y ouvrir un garage. L'expansion de son entreprise le força à se déplacer à nouveau et en 1912 il s'installa définitivement à Cowley (à six kilomètres à l'Est d'Oxford). Morris Motors était né, ancêtre du géant de l'automobile britannique, British Leyland. William Morris, devenu Lord Nuffield, utilisa une partie de sa fortune à des fins charitables et fut un grand bienfaiteur de la ville. L'existence d'un grand complexe industriel si près de la vieille ville

Unterkunftsnöte. Nordoxford in Richtung Banbury und Woodstock wurde Hauptgegend für die Neusiedlungen. Hätten Dons schon 100 Jahre eher heiraten dürfen, wäre Nordoxford ein zweites Bath geworden. Stattdessen erhielt es ein typisches viktorianisches Aussehen mit seinen großen, roten Ziegelsteinhäusern und Gärten. Nach einer Anordnung jener Zeit mußte jeder Garten mindestens zwei blühende Bäume haben. Daher ist Nordoxford heute im Frühling ein einziges Blütenmeer.

Die Geburt William Morris 1877 in Oxford sollte für die Stadt weitreichende Folgen haben. Als junger Mann eroffnete er in der High Street ein Reparaturgeschäft für Fahrräder. 1898 zog er in einen größeren Laden um und eröffnete die Morrisgaragen. 1912 zog er nach Cowley sechs Kilometer östlich von Oxford und gründete Morris Motors, die bald zu dem Riesenkonzern British Leyland anwuchsen. Der Riesenindustriekomplex nahe der Stadt bewirkte große Probleme, die durch zu späte Umweltplanung nicht mehr bewältigt werden konnten. Der Bedarf von Wohnungen und Häusern für die Fabrikarbeiter von Cowley hat weite Grünflächen Oxfords verschlungen. Die mittelalterliche Stadt erstickte fast an dem Zustrom von Einkäufern und dem Durchgangsverkehr. Das Schaffen von Umgehungs- und Einbahnstraßen hat das Problem erheblich gemildert.

Obwohl weite Gegenden Oxfords zu Wohngegenden geworden sind, ist die landschaftliche Schönheit um die Flüsse Themse und Cherwell erhalten geblieben. Port Meadow ist ein Überbleibsel des mittelalterlichen Oxford, eine große Weide auf der die Bürger ihr Vieh grasen ließen. Das Cherwelltal ist ebenfalls erhalten geblieben und seine grüne Weite reicht bis zur Innenstadt, wo sie sich an die Universitätsparks und die Wiesen von Magdalen und Christ Church College anschließt.

posa néanmoins de graves problèmes au niveau de l'environnement. Les banlieues industrielles se développèrent rapidement et les anciennes rues du centre menacèrent d'être submergées par une circulation intense. Des mesures ont été prises pour la sauvegarde des quartiers historiques ainsi que des espaces verts tels que University Parks et Christ Church Meadow.

Malgré l'urbanisation d'Oxford et de sa région, les bords de la Tamise et de la Cherwell offrent encore au visiteur les beautés reposantes de la nature. Port Meadow, par exemple, vaste espace vert situé sur la rive Est de la Tamise, est le descendant des pâturages des citoyens d'Oxford au Moyen-Age. De même, les berges de la Cherwell fournissent encore un rempart pour la vieille ville, non pas contre les invasions mais contre les dangers de l'urbanisation.

In 1854 erst bewirkte ein königlicher Untersuchungsausschuß, daß Universitätslehrer, auch „Dons" genannt, heiraten durften. Dadurch entstanden neue

A Centre of Scholarship

Throughout its history Oxford has been no quiet backwater; and in the world of scholarship it has been a main force in the thought of Britain and beyond. As an eminent historian has written, 'it is no exaggeration to say that medieval philosophy was Oxford philosophy.' The leading figure of learning in England in the first half of the thirteenth century was an Oxford scholar, Robert Grosseteste, who became Bishop of Lincoln and Chancellor of the University in 1235. He founded his philosophy on natural science, the fundamental position of mathematics and optics and the theory of light. He was the pioneer of experimental science and the reform of the calendar. His work was carried on by Roger Bacon and bore further fruit in the achievement of Richard of Wallingford, who designed the intricate astronomical clock at St Albans and compiled the first comprehensive medieval treatise on trigonometry. The tradition of philosophy combined with mathematics, astronomy and physics continued at Oxford throughout the fifteenth and sixteenth centuries and shone brilliantly in the work of Thomas Harriot, who became an Oxford B.A. in 1580. He had a great influence on algebra, optics and astronomy and connected the scientific achievements of the Middle Ages to the seventeenth century when England entered into a great scientific renaissance.

Although Isaac Newton at Cambridge was the most brilliant of the scientists of that period, it was at Oxford that this scientific renaissance originated and produced the widest results. Robert Hooke's insight into the question of circular motion 'put Newton on the track to universal gravitation'. In his laboratory in the High Street Robert Boyle evolved his 'law of gas expansion which gave birth to the age of steam' and Edmund Halley's work destroyed earlier beliefs and ushered in a new age of astronomy. Christopher Wren, an undergraduate at Wadham, is best remembered as an architect, perhaps the greatest produced by England, but he was also a scientist and friend of all the major scientists of the age. From his inspiration sprang a movement more influential in the life of Britain than St Paul's and his other architectural masterpieces – the Royal Society, the creation of a group of mainly Oxford scientists and physicians. In the following century the Rev. Gilbert White, an undergraduate at Oriel, the author of *The Natural History of Selborne*, became the unsurpassed pioneer of the meticulous study of nature.

In the later seventeenth century the dominant figure in medical research was Thomas Sydenham, who became an undergraduate in 1647, and medical research has always held a high place in the scientific life of Oxford. It was in London that Alexander Fleming discovered penicillin, but it was H. W. Florey and his group of researchers at Oxford who turned that discovery to practical use and applied it to a human patient in 1941. Under the leadership of C. S. Sherington from Cambridge, who became the Waynflete Professor of Physiology, Oxford made the greatest contribution to the study of neurophysiology at the beginning of the present century. Since then the list of Nobel Prizewinners, including Hinshelwood, Robinson, Krebs and Porter, testifies to the eminence of the Chemistry and Biochemistry Schools; and the work of Dorothy Hodgkins is the most significant achievement of crystallography.

In politics Oxford has held a dominant position. Almost half of the Prime Ministers of the United Kingdom and a high proportion of the Ministers of State have been Oxford graduates and in literature the list of great writers is long. The chief philosophers of the seventeenth century, Locke and Hobbes, were Oxford men as was Dr Johnson, the father of lexicography and hub of the literary society of the later eighteenth century. The Oxford University Press has carried on his work and the *Oxford Dictionary* is the foremost dictionary of the English language. In *The Decline and Fall of the Roman Empire* Edmund Gibbon produced what is perhaps the most famous book of history in the English-speaking world. At the same time appeared Blackstone's *Commentaries on the Laws of England*, one of the most influential legal books ever written, and in 1776, the year in which Gibbon published the first volume of *The Decline and Fall*, Adam Smith's *The Wealth of*

John Tradescant (d. 1637), gardener to Charles II and traveller, began the collection which his son John bequeathed to Elias Ashmole, and which formed the basis of the Ashmolean Museum (portraits by courtesy of Oxfordshire County Libraries).

La base de la collection du musée Ashmolean provient d'un don de Elias Ashmole qui la tenait de John Tradescant (mort en 1637) grand voyageur et jardinier du roi Charles II.

John Tradescant (gest. 1637), Gärtner für Karl II. und Reisender, begann eine Sammlung, die sein Sohn Elias Ashmole hinterließ und die der Grundstein für das Ashmolean Museum wurde.

Overleaf: *The Ashmolean Museum, by Frederick Mackenzie* (by courtesy of the Ashmolean Museum, Oxford). ▶
Au verso: Le musée Ashmolean, par Frederick Mackenzie.
Umseitig: Das Ashmolean Museum von Frederick Mackenzie.

Nations appeared and gave birth to the science of economics.

The English language owes much to the exquisite writing of Walter Pater and Froude, of Addison, Ruskin and other Oxford authors, and among poets are numbered Shelley and Swinburne, Matthew Arnold and Bridges and Auden. Religion has been deeply affected by Oxford. From Christ Church came John and Charles Wesley, from whose teaching grew the worldwide Methodist Church, while the Oxford, or Tractarian, Movement, which profoundly affected the Anglican Church both in England and throughout the world, sprang from John Keble's sermon on 'national apostasy', preached in the University Church in 1833.

It is strange that Matthew Arnold, an Oxford man and great lover of his university, should have called Oxford a 'home of lost causes'. She has in fact been a pioneer and leader in science and the arts, in religion and politics, a home not of lost causes but of intellectual progress.

Happily the enmity between Town and Gown, the city and the University, has been conquered by mutual understanding and goodwill after so many centuries of University dominance. Let us leave the last word to a Frenchman. In a biography of Cecil Rhodes who, as a very young man, made a vast fortune in the diamond mines of South Africa and then came to Oxford as an undergraduate at Oriel, André Maurois remarked on the strange experience of coming 'from the law of the jungle to the most civilised city in the world'.

Charles Lutwidge Dodgson (1832–98), better known as Lewis Carroll, was a mathematics lecturer at Oxford. He wrote Alice in Wonderland *in 1865, basing* Alice **(below)** *on the daughter of Dean Liddell of Christ Church* (portrait by courtesy of the Governing Body, Christ Church, Oxford).
Charles L. Dodgson (alias Lewis Carroll) enseignait les mathématiques à Oxford. Il écrivit Alice aux Pays des Merveilles **(ci-dessous)** *en 1865 d'après Alice Liddell, fille du doyen de Christ Church.*
Charles Lutwidge Dodgson bekannter unter dem Namen Lewis Carroll, war Mathematikprofessor in Oxford. Er schrieb Alice in Wonderland *im Jahre 1865, wobei er die Tochter des Dekan Liddell von Christ Church zum Vorwurf für Alice **(unten)** nahm.*

🇫🇷 Oxford a toujours été à la pointe du progrès intellectuel et de la pensée britanniques. Ainsi que le fit remarquer un éminent historien « il n'est pas exagéré d'affirmer que la philosophie du moyen-âge était la philosophie d'Oxford ». Son premier représentant de marque au XIIIe siècle fut Robert Grosseteste, dont l'œuvre fut poursuivie par Roger Bacon, puis Richard de Wallingford, auteur du premier traité complet de trigonométrie. Les savants d'Oxford continuèrent cette tradition alliant la philosophie aux mathématiques, à l'astronomie et à la physique pendant les XVe et XVIe siècles, avec particulièrement Thomas Harriot, diplomé d'Oxford en 1580, qui devait avoir une grande influence sur l'algèbre, l'optique et l'astronomie et la renaissance scientifique de l'Angleterre au XVIIe siècle.

Bien qu'Isaac Newton, savant le plus célèbre de cette époque, ait été à Cambridge, c'est bien à Oxford que cette renaissance se développa, avec en particulier les travaux de Robert Hooke, Robert Boyle et Edmund Halley. Christopher Wren, le célèbre architecte, auteur en particulier de la cathédrale St Paul's, étudia a Wadham College et fut l'instigateur de la célèbre et puissante Royal Society.

Vers la fin du XVIIe siècle Oxford devint également un grand centre de la recherche médicale, avec en particulier Thomas Sydenham. C'est aussi grâce aux travaux de H. W. Florey à Oxford que la pénicilline (découverte par Fleming) put être appliquée aux humains en 1941.

La liste de savants d'Oxford titulaires du prix Nobel est impressionnante (avec en particulier Hinshelwood, Robinson, Krebs et Porter) et les travaux de Dorothy Hodgkins furent essentiels pour la cristallographie.

Oxford tient également sa place dans le monde de la politique et peut se vanter d'avoir formé près de la moitié des premiers ministres et ministres d'état britanniques. Les grands philosophes du XVIIe siècle, Locke et Hobbes, étudièrent à Oxford ainsi que le Dr Johnson, ancêtre de la lexicographie. Le célèbre *Oxford Dictionary* est d'ailleurs l'œuvre maîtresse dans son domaine. Parmi les grands savants du XVIIIe siècle, citons l'historien Gibbon, le juriste Blackstone et l'économiste Adam Smith.

Oxford a naturellement ses romanciers, essayistes et poètes; parmi les plus célèbres on peut citer Ruskin, Shelley, Swinburne, Matthew Arnold, Bridges et Auden. Les théologiens d'Oxford influencèrent profondément la religion en Grande-Bretagne et notamment John et Charles Wesley, pères du culte méthodiste et John Keble, instigateur du mouvement d'Oxford, dit *Tractarian*, qui influença beaucoup l'église anglicane.

Pour résumer le rôle d'Oxford dans les sphères culturelles et intellectuelles, on ne pourrait mieux faire que de citer André Maurois qui, dans sa biographie de Cecil Rhodes (qui, jeune homme, fit sa fortune dans les diamants en Afrique du Sud puis alla étudier à Oxford) rapporte l'expression de celui-ci « la ville la plus civilisée du monde ».

Im Bereich der Wissenschaft war Oxford für Großbritannien und andere Länder wegweisend. Ein eminenter Gelehrter in England zu Beginn des 13. Jh. war der Oxforder Robert Grosseteste, im Jahr 1235 Bischof von Lincoln und Rektor der Universität. Er begründete eine Philosophie der Naturwissenschaften, schrieb über die fundamentale Stellung der Mathematik, der Optik und eine Lichttheorie. Roger Bacon und Richard Wallingford setzten seine Arbeit fort. Letzterer stellte die erste umfassende mittelalterliche Abhandlung über Trigonometrie zusammen. Die Tradition der Kombination von Philosophie, Mathematik, Astronomie und Physik wurde in Oxford im 15. und 16. Jh. fortgesetzt und zeigte sich am großartigsten in Thomas Harriot, der die wissenschaftlichen Errungenschaften des Mittelalters in das 17. Jh. brachte, in dem England eine große wissenschaftliche Renaissance erlebte.

Obwohl Isaac Newton, der brillianteste Wissenschaftler dieser Zeit, in Cambridge wirkte, nahm die wissenschaftliche Renaissance ihren Anfang in Oxford und hatte die größten Ergebnisse. Robert Boyle entwickelte hier sein „Gesetz der Gasausdehnung", das der Beginn des Dampfzeitalters wurde und Edmund Halley's Arbeit brachte völlig neue Erkenntnisse in der Astronomie. Christopher Wren ist hauptsächlich als Architekt bekannt, aber er war auch Wissenschaftler. Der Pfarrer Gilbert White, Author der *Naturgeschichte von Selborne* wurde unübertroffener Pionier in der exakten Naturkunde.

Die beherrschende Figur im späten 17. Jh. auf dem Gebiet der medizinischen Forschung war Thomas Sydenham. Alexander Fleming entdeckte das Penizillin zwar in London, aber H. W. Florey und sein Forschungsteam wandten diese Entdeckung 1941 zum ersten Mal praktisch in Oxford an. Unter der Führung von C. S. Sherington von Cambridge steuerte Oxford seinen größten Beitrag im Studium der Neurophysiologie bei. Die Liste von Nobelpreisträgern wie Hinshelwood, Robinson, Krebs und Porter verweist auf die hervorragende Stellung der Chemie- und Biochemieschulen Oxfords. Dorothy Hodgkins Arbeit auf dem Gebiet der Kristallographie ist eine der bedeutendsten Leistungen.

Auch in der Politik hielt Oxford

Christ Church Cathedral is the smallest cathedral in England and is also the College Chapel. The Choir, shown here, has beautiful Perpendicular fan vaulting.
Christ Church est la plus petite cathédrale d'Angleterre et sert de chapelle au collège. On peut admirer ici les voûtes du chœur, décorées en style « perpendiculaire ».
Die Christ Church Kathedrale ist Englands kleinste Kathedrale und auch College Kapelle. Der hier sichtbare Chor hat wunderschöne spätgotische Gewölbe.

eine dominierende Stellung inne. Fast die Hälfte aller britischen Premierminister und ein hoher Anteil Minister waren Oxford Studenten. Auf dem Gebiet der Literatur ist die Liste großer Schriftsteller lang. Die größten Philosophen des 17. Jahrhunderts Locke und Hobbes waren von Oxford, ebenso Dr. Johnson, Vater der Lexikographie. Die Oxford University Press führte seine Arbeit fort und das *Oxford Wörterbuch* ist das führende Wörterbuch der englischen Sprache. Mit seinem *Niedergang und Fall des Römischen Reiches* schrieb Edmund Gibbon wohl das berühmteste Geschichtswerk der englischsprechenden Welt. Blackstones *Kommentare über das Gesetz Englands* stellt überhaupt eines der einflußreichsten Rechtsbücher dar. Im Jahre 1776 erschien Adam Smiths Buch *Der Reichtum der Nationen*, das Wegweiser der Wirtschaftswissenschaften wurde.

Berühmte Schriftsteller und Dichter Oxfords waren Walter Pater und Froude, Addison, Ruskin, sowie Shelley und Swinburne, Matthew Arnold, Bridges und Auden. Auf dem Gebiet der Religion wären John und Charles Wesley zu erwähnen, sowie John Keble.

Die jahrhundertelange Feindseligkeit zwischen Stadt und Universität ist glücklicherweise durch den guten Willen beider Parteien behoben.

Traditional Oxford

Above left and below: *For over three hundred years a fair has been held at the beginning of September in St Giles and now, although St Giles is a wide, main thoroughfare with colleges and houses, on the first Monday and Tuesday of September every year, from side to side and end to end, there are booths, roundabouts and all the paraphernalia of a modern amusement fair and access is impossible* except by foot. Tradition is more important than inconvenience caused to those who live there (fair picture by courtesy of Oxfordshire County Libraries).

Above right: *at sunrise on 1 May each year the choir of Magdalen College sings a hymn from the top of the Great Tower, while crowds throng the High to hear them* (by courtesy of Oxfordshire County Libraries).

Ci-dessus à droite: le 1er mai de chaque année, à l'aube, la chorale de Magdalen College chante du haut de la Grande Tour pour la foule amassée dans « the High ».

Ci-dessus à gauche, et ci-dessous: *Le premier lundi et mardi de septembre, tous les ans, une fête foraine s'installe dans St Giles, artère importante de la ville, bordée de collèges.*

Oben links und unten: *Im Stadtteil von St. Giles findet seit über drei Jahhunderten alljährlich am 1. Montag und Dienstag im September eine Kirmes statt.*

Oben rechts: *Jedes Jahr am 1. Mai singt der Chor des Magdalenen College eine Hymne vom Großturm, wobei sich eine große Menschenmenge in der High Street ansammelt und zuhört.*